KWANZAA

Songs For Everyone

Karen Griner Smith

authorHOUSE®

AuthorHouse™
1663 Liberty Drive
Bloomington, IN 47403
www.authorhouse.com
Phone: 1-800-839-8640

First published by AuthorHouse   01/06/2012

ISBN: 978-1-4685-4140-3 (sc)
ISBN: 978-1-4685-4139-7 (ebk)

Printed in the United States of America

Any people depicted in stock imagery provided by Thinkstock are models, and such images are being used for illustrative purposes only.
Certain stock imagery © Thinkstock.

This book is printed on acid-free paper.

Table of Contents

To Everette Griner, my father, whose passing during Kwanzaa
inspired these songs;

To Rashard, Savannah and Amir Brown, my grandchildren,
who are inspirational by just being themselves;

And to Deborah Griner Randall, my sister, who planted the idea of music
for Kwanzaa that school children could sing.

Introduction

Jingle Bells. Silent Night. Oh Come All Ye Faithful. Joy To the World. I just love Christmas music! I grew up on it. It evokes feelings of happiness, love, and good times. I play it all year round whenever my spirits need a boost.

I also love Kwanzaa, the harvest feast period celebrated by many African-Americans. It is a holiday that honors and respects the past, present and future of my people. I am attracted to Kwanzaa's focus on family activities, community spirit, and promotion of togetherness, idea sharing, and creativity.

One day it occurred to me that I could have my cake and eat it, too. I combined the music of Christmas and the ideology of Kwanzaa into Kwanzaa Songs!!!!!!!! A small number of the songs are set to universally familiar tunes, which are not traditional Christmas music. These songs belong in this collection because the lyrics evoke the cultural awareness and happy experience that is Kwanzaa.

I have three wishes. The first is that all who sing these songs enjoy them as much as I do to add musical spice to Kwanzaa celebrations everywhere. The second is that these songs help facilitate the spread of the Kwanzaa celebration further into the mainstream of African-American culture. The third is that children in schools will sing these songs during the winter holiday season.

We already know the tunes. Now let us embrace the new lyrics with the peace, joy and love of the season. Through these songs may the spirit of Kwanzaa, be enjoyed by the family, sung in schools, and shared with the entire community!

Karen Griner Smith

Word-Sounding Glossary

Ashe—(ah-SHAY)—Spiritual thanks
Habari gani—(HA-bar-ree GA-nee)—What's the news? What's new today?
Harumbee—(Ha-RUM-beh)—All pull together
Imani—(ee-MAH-nee)—Faith; day seven of Kwanzaa
Karamu—(ka-RAH-moo)—Feast
Kikombe Cha Umoja—(key-COM-bey CHA oo-MO-jah)—Unity cup
Kinara—(kee-NAH-rah)—Candle holder
Kujichagulia—(koo-gee-cha-goo-LEE-yah)—Self determination; day two of Kwanzaa
Kuumba—Kuumba (koo-OOM-bah)—Creativity; day five of Kwanzaa
Kutoa Majina—(koo-TOE-ah mah-GEE-nah)—calling the names of family ancestors and great heroes
Kwanzaa—(KWAN-zah)—Harvest celebration
Mazeo—(ma-ZAY-oh)—crops; fruits and vegetables
Mishumaa Saba—(mee-shoo-MAH SAH-bah)—Seven principles
Mkeka—(em-KEH-kah)—Straw mat
Muhindi—(moo-HIN-dee)—Corn
Ngoma—(n-GO-mah)—drums
Nguzo Saba—(n-GOO-zo SAH-bah)—the seven guiding principles on which Kwanzaa is based
Nia—(NEE-yah))—Purpose; day six of Kwanzaa
Tambiko—(tahm-BEE-ko)—pouring libation to honor the ancestors
Tamshi la Tutaonana—(TAHM-shee LA too-tah-oh-NAH-nah)—farewell statement
Ujamaa—(oo-JAH-mah)—Cooperative economics; day four of Kwanzaa
Ujima—(oo-GEE-mah)—Collective works and responsibility; day three of Kwanzaa
Umoja—(oo-MO-jah)—Unity; day one of Kwanzaa
Vibunzi—(vee-BOON-zee)—ears of corn
Zawadi—(za-WAH-dee)—Presents; gifts

Tips on Swahili pronounciation.
- Consonants are pronounced like English consonants.
- The "R" is like the Spanish "R" and is pronounced by rolling the tongue.
- In most Swahili words, the accent is placed on the next-to-last syllable.
- Swahili vowels are pronounced as follows: a (ah), e (ay), I (ee), o (oe), u (oo).

The Kwanzaa Experience

When I was a child back in the '50's and '60's my family had gatherings. Adults and children would get together and party! We laughed, danced, sang, ate and talked together. The adults would give the youngsters a nickel or quarter to show them the latest dance steps. We children would listen to the tales older folks told about how life was in their younger days. Their experiences were foreign to us and we eagerly listened. They described historical conditions in ways that helped us to better understand those times. They spoke of relatives who had passed on whom we never knew before, but whom we came to know through the information that our parents and relatives shared with us. In this way the generations became linked.

This was how I learned many important facts, like my mother's relatives were descendants of Robert E. Lee's slaves. We did not have many material things in those days, but we didn't need them. We had love, respect and each other. In celebrating Kwanzaa, I found the spirit and love of those "good old days."

The word "Kwanzaa" comes from the Swahili language, as do all the terms used in the celebration. Kwanzaa means "the first fruits of harvest". It is celebrated during the seven-day period from December 26 to January 1. In 1966 Dr. Maulana Ron Karenga developed the idea of Kwanzaa so that African Americans could have a way to incorporate our heritage into festivities of the winter holiday season. After nearly forty years in practice, Kwanzaa has grown to become a worldwide celebration experienced by over five million people though out America, the African Diaspora, and all over the world.

The Kwanzaa celebration brings forth personal pride and community appreciation. It is a unique event that pays homage to the past, present and future. Through family discussions elders share their wisdom and share important information with younger generations. The younger generation, in turn, share with the elders what is happening now. These communications cross age roadblocks to bring about mutual respect for all those involved.

People may experience Kwanzaa in public gatherings, but most Kwanzaa activities occur in private homes with family and friends. Celebrants go to a different person's house each night of the week. Many are unable to attend daily events, but participate as often as possible, even if it is for only one or two nights of activities. The family and friends attending a Kwanzaa celebration generally bring a dish or beverage to contribute to the feast, but it is not a necessity. People may dress in African clothing if they have them, but this also is not a necessity. The most important thing is to attend an event and experience the spirit of Kwanzaa.

Although the general set-up and principles are the same, the actual celebration is fluid and may be modified to suit individual taste and practices. Generally, after the more solemn agendas of lighting the candles, paying respect to the ancestors and discussing the principle of the night have been observed, Kwanzaa usually evolves into a gathering where people eat, laugh, dance, sing, and socialize. The other elements of the celebration are open to personal choice.

The seven principles promote the growth of a cooperative community spirit, cooperative economic opportunities, interpersonal cooperation, and individual advancement. Although discussed during the Kwanzaa season, the ultimate goal is that the Nguzo Saba (the Seven Principles) become a living part of the individual and community until they are practiced every day of the year.

Preparation for Kwanzaa

Decorate for Kwanzaa to create an atmosphere with an African flavor by using natural materials and homemade items. Move away from commercialization. Decorations may be simple or elaborate. They may include prints of African art, original African art, masks and sculpture, drums or other African articles.

Fabric with African design may be draped for a dramatic effect. Red, black and green are the colors of Kwanzaa and should be included. The focal point of the room is the kinara and other symbols of Kwanzaa. The following are the only "must haves" to conduct a Kwanzaa ceremony:

A straw mat called the Mkeka. Place the items needed on it. A place mat made of straw, sticks, cloth or other natural fibers is suggested.

A candleholder called a Kinara to hold seven candles. It is made out of wood, and may be crafted in any simple way to hold seven candles safely. A simple one may be made by taking a piece of flat wood long enough to hold seven candles and banging seven long nails until they protrude through to hold the candles.

Seven candles—One black, three red, three green. The black candle is always placed in the middle the three red ones to the left and three green ones to the right. The colors have special meaning: black to represent our people; red to represent the blood of our ancestors; green to represent the land of our ancestors—Mother Africa. If black candles are hard to find, any candle may be colored with a black marker or black shoe polish.

A unity cup—called the Kikombe Cha Umoja. We pour libations to honor our ancestors and share a drink with others in a gesture of togetherness. Choose a special cup that has been in your family or one that is made from some natural material such as wood, pottery or gourd.

Clean water—It is used in pouring libation and drinking from the unity cup. A slightly different practice is to pour water onto the floor in the four comers of the room to represent the four cardinal points of the globe. After the libation, fill the unity cup once more and pass it so each person may take a sip or a symbolic sip as a sign of unity.

Whichever libation type is selected, the end is the same. The group shouts in unison the word "Harumbee" seven times, which means "let's pull together". The seventh pronunciation should be yelled loud and last as long as the group can carry it.

The fruits of the harvest—called the Mazao, are fruits, nuts, and gourds. This includes ears of dried corn called Muhindi or Vibunzi. The ears represent the number of children in the host family's household. If there is not enough; the ears may be broken up so the pieces equal the number of children born to that home. If there are no children, one ear is displayed as a symbolic representation of future generations. Place the Mazao in a wooden bowl or a basket, or arrange them on the mkeka (straw mat) around the kinara.

Handmade gifts and presents—called Zawadi. One may purchase gifts, but handmade ones are preferred. These gifts do not have to be perfectly crafted or expensive. They are unique and have special meaning because we made them ourselves. They can be intangible, like a song or a dance or a foot rub. They are personal expressions of love.

Celebration of Kwanzaa

1. We greet each other with "Habari gani?" which means, "What's the news?" The answer is the principle for that night. The first day's answer is Umoja, the second is Kujichagulia, etc.) The seven principles are:

   - Day One—Umoja (oo-MO-jah) means unity; This is the foundation principle of Kwanzaa. We can do together what we cannot do alone. It sets the tone for a week of peace, harmony and togetherness.

   - Day Two—Kujichagulia (koo-gee-cha-goo-LEE-yah) means self-determination. We have the right and responsibility define ourselves and make decisions in our own best interest concerning self, our families and our community. We are not limited to someone else's idea of who we are or what we should be.

   - Day three—Ujima (oo-GEE-mah) means collective works and responsibility. This principle encourages solving problems through teamwork, and a responsibility to our immediate and world communities.

   - Day Four—Ujamaa (oo-JAH-mah) means cooperative economics. This principle encourages building economic strength in our communities. We do this by supporting each other's business efforts, using products and services from African American providers, and sharing opportunities for economic growth.

   - Day Five—Nia (NEE-yah) means purpose. This principle helps us to understand ourselves on personal and community levels. We learn to understand our motivations and how our actions affect one another.

   - Day Six—Kuumba (koo-OOM-bah) means creativity. We learn to use education and talents to benefit ourselves and the community. We learn to use old things in a new ways and reveal our hidden talents.

   - Day Seven—Imani (ee-MAH-nee) means faith. We come from a strong tradition of faith. It helps us to survive many obstacles. Faith is needed to maintain positive energy and to continue forward movement.

2. We ask the oldest person in the room "Do we have your permission to begin this celebration?" We do this as a sign of respect for the elders. Permission is given with a simple, "Yes, you have my permission" Then the activities may begin.

3. Each night we light a candle. We begin with the black one in the center. This candle is lit first every night and used to light the others. On the second night a red one candle is lit. On the third night the two candles which were lit before are re-lit and a green one is added. Each night all the previous candles are re-lit and an additional candle is lit, alternating red and green, until all seven are ablaze on night seven. If the room is darkened for this activity, the lighting ceremony is more dramatic.

4. We pass the unity cup. We pour libation (tambiko) to ancestors and encourage everyone to pay respect to those they choose to remember in this activity (family members, friends, or famous people who have passed on). Say the name of the person remembered while pouring a few drops of water from the unity cup. The water should fall into a plant or a tub and used to water plants later. A container of extra water should be close by so the cup may be refilled if needed.

5. We announce the principle of the day and discuss it to the best of our ability. All persons present state their belief on the principle of the day. This may or may not lead to more extended conversations among guests. The host may also choose to have a guest speaker to discuss or teach about the topic of the day.

6. We exchange home crafted gifts. Gifts are traditionally given on January 1, Imani, the last day of Kwanzaa. However, they may be given at any time. If multiple gifts are given, one each night, the most meaningful gift is given on night seven.

7. We share in a Karamu. Usually this fun and feasting is a pot-luck meal where visitors bring a dish to share with others. The most elaborate feast is held on day six; however, a karamu may be held on any day of Kwanzaa.

8. Rejoicing takes place after the meal. People have an intergenerational party family style. Visual artists, jewelry makers, people who sew, etc. may put their work on display. Those with performing talents like singing, dancing, rapping, reciting poetry, telling jokes, etc. share them in impromptu performances. We also have "jam" sessions where everyone joins in singing popular songs or holiday tunes, with African musical instruments, such as drums and shakers, or home made instruments like a pot and a wooden spoon. You may choose to play group games, such as charades. If so, it is good to suggest cultural themes to maintain the spirit of Kwanzaa.

The celebration often ends with visitors joining together in a circle for group prayer or words of encouragement to recommit their efforts to serve the community and follow the seven principles of Kwanzaa.

"Ashe! Peace and Blessings!"

A Special Celebration

Tune: The Holly and the Ivy

Lyrics: Karen Griner Smith

1700's

The Kwan-zaa ce - le - bra - tion that hap-pens ev' - ry year
At/this - spe - cial time called Kwan - zaa we learn our her - i - tage
At/this spe - cial ce - le - bra - tion we remem-ber ev' - ry one

is a time of fun for - ev' - ry one full of laugh-ter and of cheer.
we - do not ne - glect we_ give re - spect to all peo - ple e' - ry age.
like the memo-ries of those that we love our an - ces-tors who've passed on.

It was Doctor-Ron Ka - ran - ga in nine-teen six - ty six
The se - ven days of Kwan-zaa we have can - dles/that we light
Come join the ce - le - bra - tion where friends and fam - ily bring

Who de - signed the ways to en - joy these days so we all could be - ne - fit.
Through the nei - bor-hood we_ share much good and our thoughts are clean and bright.
tas - ty things to eat, lots of fruits and meat, then we laugh and dance and sing.

Celebrate our Culture
Tune: Angels We Have Heard On High

Traditional, 1700's

Lyrics: Karen Griner Smith

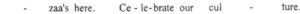

Come and Feel the Love
Tune: Joy To the World

George F. Handel

Lyrics: Karen Griner Smith

Come To the Table
Tune: O Come All Ye Faithful John Reading, 1751

Lyrics: Karen Griner Smith

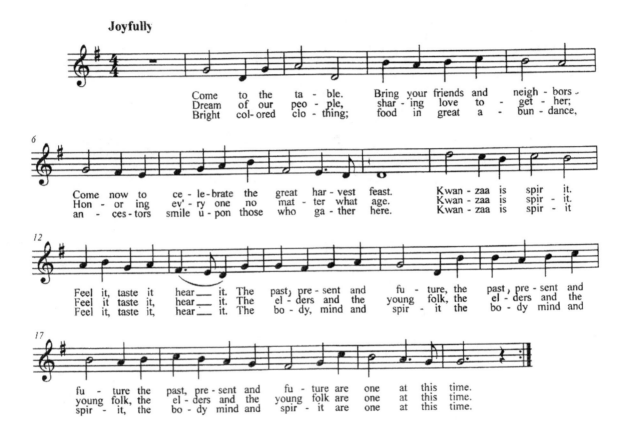

Joyfully

Come to the ta - ble. Bring your friends and neigh - bors
Dream of our peo - ple, shar - ing love to - get - her;
Bright col- ored clo - thing; food in great a - bun - dance,

Come now to ce - le - brate the great har - vest feast. Kwan - zaa is spir it.
Hon - or ing ev' - ry one no mat - ter what age. Kwan - zaa is spir - it.
an - ces-tors smile u - pon those who ga - ther here. Kwan - zaa is spir - it

Feel it, taste it hear __ it. The past, pre - sent and fu - ture, the past, pre - sent and
Feel it taste it, hear __ it. The el - ders and the young folk, the el - ders and the
Feel it, taste it, hear __ it. The bo - dy, mind and spir - it the bo - dy mind and

fu - ture the past, pre - sent and fu - ture are one at this time.
young folk, the el - ders and the young folk are one at this time.
spir - it, the bo - dy mind and spir - it are one at this time.

The Days of Kwanzaa Time
Tune: Auld Lang Syne

Robert Burns

Lyrics: Karen Griner Smith

Moderately

Lest our an-ces-tors be for-got and nev-ver brought to mind, we
We share the fruits of har-vest feast and with happi-ness we hear The
We have this har-vest ho-li-day to enhance our u-ni-ty. The

think of them with love and praise in days of Kwan-zaa time. For se-ven days we
wis-dom of our el-ders in our hearts and in our ears. " " " " " "
love for peo-ple in our homes flows to our com-mun-ity. " " " " " "

speak of peace our se-ven can-dles shine We con-gre-gate to ce-le-brate the
" " " " " " " " " " " " " " " "

days of Kwan-zaa time.
" " " " "

Harumbee! Kwanzaa's Here

Tune: Kum Bah Yah

Lyrics: Karen Griner Smith

Spiritual

Can - dles all burn bright, Kwan - zaa's here! Ev' - ry
Things worth think - ing of, Kwan - zaa's here! Ho - nor
Share the har - vest feast, Kwan - zaa's here! Love and
Growth and u - ni - ty, Kwan - zaa's here! Serve com -

one de - lights, Kwan - zaa's here! Drums beat through the
those we love, Kwan - zaa's here! Praise to God a -
joy in - crease, Kwan - zaa's here! Un - cle, aunt and
mu - ni - ty, Kwan - zaa's here! Show hu - man - i -

night, Kwan - zaa's here! Ha - rum - bee, Kwan - zaa's
bove, Kwan - zaa's here! Ha - rum - bee, Kwan - zaa's
niece, Kwan - zaa's here! Ha - rum - bee! Kwan - zaa's
ty, Kwan - zaa's here! Ha - rum - bee Kwan - zaa's

here! Red and black and green, Kwan - zaa's here!
here! Learn our his - tor - y Kwan - zaa's here!
here! Share what we cre - ate, Kwan - zaa's here!
here! Love for ev - ery - one, Kwan - zaa's here!

Thoughts are pure and clean, Kwan - zaa's here! Raise your
Learn what you can be, Kwan - zaa's here! Pride for
Laugh and ce - le - brate, Kwan - zaa's here! Talk and
Hap - pi - ness and fun, Kwan - zaa's here! Kwan - zaa

self es - teem, - Kwan - zaa's here! Ha - rum - bee!
all to see, Kwan - zaa's here! Ha - rum - bee!
con - ver - sate, Kwan - zaa's here! Ha - rum - bee!
has be - gun, Kwan - zaa's here! Ha - rum - bee!

Kwan - zaa's here!
Kwan - zaa's here!
Kwan - zaa's here!
Kwan - zaa's here!

Kwanzaa
Tune: Deck the Halls

Ancient Welsh Tune

Lyrics: Karen Griner Smith

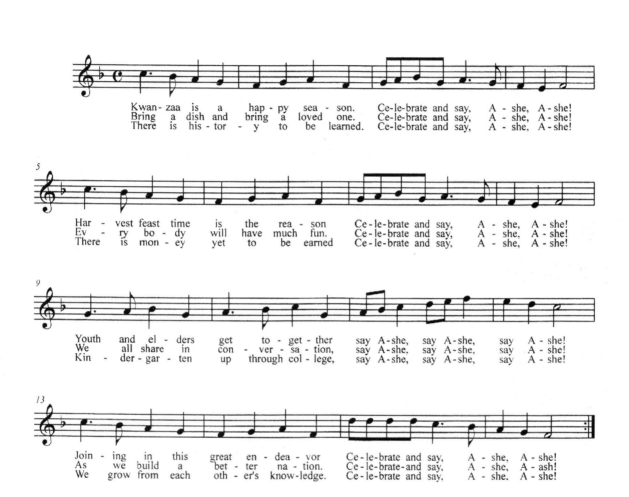

Kwan - zaa is a hap - py sea - son. Ce - le - brate and say, A - she, A - she!
Bring a dish and bring a loved one. Ce - le - brate and say, A - she, A - she!
There is his - tor - y to be learned. Ce - le - brate and say, A - she, A - she!

Har - vest feast time is the rea - son Ce - le - brate and say, A - she, A - she!
Ev - ry bo - dy will have much fun. Ce - le - brate and say, A - she, A - she!
There is mon - ey yet to be earned Ce - le - brate and say, A - she, A - she!

Youth and el - ders get to - get - ther say A-she, say A-she, say A - she!
We all share in con - ver - sa - tion, say A-she, say A-she, say A - she!
Kin - der-gar - ten up through col - lege, say A-she, say A-she, say A - she!

Join - ing in this great en - dea - vor Ce - le - brate and say, A - she, A - she!
As we build a bet - ter na - tion. Ce - le - brate-and say, A - she, A - ash!
We grow from each oth - er's know-ledge. Ce - le - brate and say, A - she, A - she!

Kwanzaa Is For Family Fun

Tune: We Three Kings of Orient Are

Lyrics: Karen Griner Smith

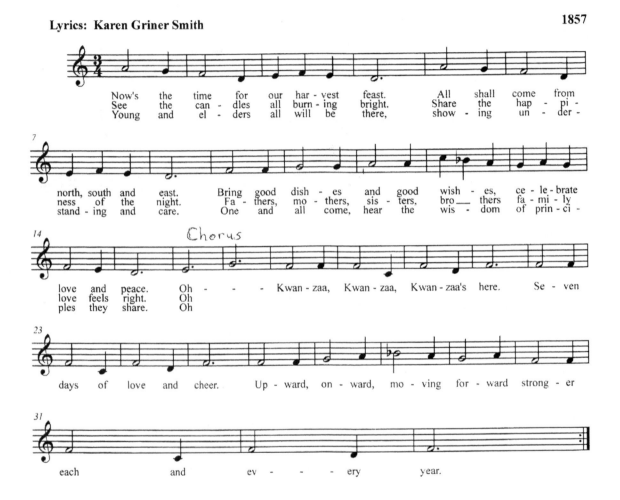

Now's the time for our har - vest feast. All shall come from
See the can - dles all burn - ing bright. Share the hap - pi -
Young and el - ders all will be there, show - ing un - der -

north, south and east. Bring good dish - es and good wish - es, ce - le - brate
ness of the night. Fa - thers, mo - thers, sis - ters, bro___ thers fa - mi - ly
stand - ing and care. One and all come, hear the wis - dom of prin - ci -

Chorus

love and peace. Oh - - Kwan - zaa, Kwan - zaa, Kwan - zaa's here. Se - ven
love feels right. Oh
ples they share. Oh

days of love and cheer. Up - ward, on - ward, mo - ving for - ward strong - er

each and ev - - ery year.

Kwanzaa Is the Name
Tune: B-I-N-G-O

Lyrics: Karen Griner Smith

Traditional

Kwanzaa Is the Time of Year

Tune: Twinkle Twinkle Little Star

Traditional

Lyrics: Karen Griner Smith

Kwan- zaa is the time of year ev' - ry one is in good cheer.
Kwan- zaa is the time of year ev' - ry one is in good cheer.
Kwan- zaa is the time of year ev' - ry one is in good cheer.

Fruits of har - vest all a - bound. Friends and fam - ily gat - her 'round.
Ho - nor to an - ces - tors who Built foun - da - tions strong and true.
Learn - ing those im - por - tant facts' Wear - ing red and green and black,

Talk of prin - ci - ples we seek. Light the can - dles. Serve the feast.
We black peo - ple ce - le - brate All the ones who make us great.
Wak - ing up our eth - nic pride To all that we are in - side.

Kwanzaa Is Coming

Children, Go Where I Send Thee

Lyrics: Karen Griner Smith

Traditional

*Sing these two measures two times for verse 2,
three times for verse 3, etc. in REVERSE order.

Similar to music pattern of song
The Twelve Days of Christmas.

KWANZAA'S HERE
Tune: Jingle Bells

J. Pierpont

Lyrics: Karen Griner Smith

Let Us Say "Ashe, Ashe"
Tune: Bring A Torch Jeanette Isabella

Lyrics: Karen Griner Smith

Traditional French

Now Is the Time
Tune: Silent Night

Franz Gruber

Lyrics: Karen Griner Smith

Reverently

Now is the time. Kwan - zaa is here.
Now is the time. Kwan - zaa is here.
Now is the time. Kwan - zaa is here.
Now is the time. Kwan - zaa is here.

Se - ven days filled with cheer.
Ga - ther your loved ones near.
Ce - le - brate. Learn to share.
Share your love. Show you care.

Se - ven can - dles will shine in the night.
Bring your friends and your fam - ly to meet.
Tell the sto - ries of pre - sent and past.
Use your gift of crea - a - ti - vi - ty

Se - ven prin - ci - ples lead us to light.
Bring the dish - es they all love to eat.
Learn to pros - per make our suc - cess last.
Ma - king pre - sents for your fa - mi - ly.

U - ni - ty has be - gun.
Share with peo - ple we love.
Strive for true u - ni - ty.
Fam - ily love is di - vine.

We as a peo - ple are one.
Prai - ses to God up a - bove.
Re - spect our com - mu - ni - ty.
Kwan - zaa's a won - der - ful time!

Our Harvest Celebration

Tune: Oh Christmas Tree

Lyrics: Karen Griner Smith

1800's Old German Carol

Chorus
It's Kwan-zaa time, it's Kwan-zaa time, Our har-vest ce - le - bra-tion. It's

Kwan-zaa time, it's Kwan-zaa time, Our har-vest ce - le - bra-tion.

Verse
De - cem - ber twen - ty
Ha - ba - ri Ga - ni?
The se - ven can - dles
The hand-made gifts, the
We drink the cup of
We place a spe - cial
We pour li - ba - tion
We share our ta - lents

six be - gins, and Jan - u - ar - y first it ends. It's Kwan-zaa time, it's
What's the news? We learn new facts, broad - en our views. " " " " "
that we light on the ki - na - ra burn so bright. " " " " "
fruit and corn, the mat of straw they sit u - pon. " " " " "
u - ni - ty, we pledge to serve com - mun - i - ty. " " " " "
ear of corn for ev' - ry child with - in the home. " " " " "
to the past; We speak of growth and fu - ture tasks. " " " " "
and our love, we give our thanks to God a - bove. " " " " "

To Chorus
Kwan-zaa time, our har-vest ce - le - bra - - - - tion.

Seven Principles of Kwanzaa
Tune: I Saw Three Ships Come Sailing In

Lyrics: Karen Griner Smith

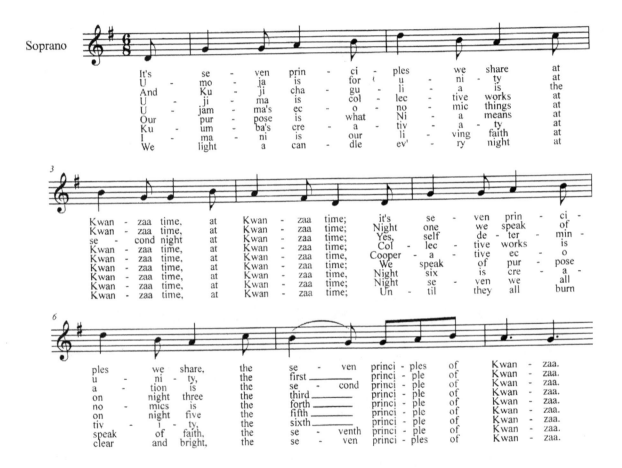

Signs of Kwanzaa

Tune: Hark The Herald Angels Sing

Lyrics: Karen Griner Smith

1855

To Celebrate Kwanzaa

Tune: Away In A Manger

Lyrics: Karen Griner Smith

Johnathan E. Spillman

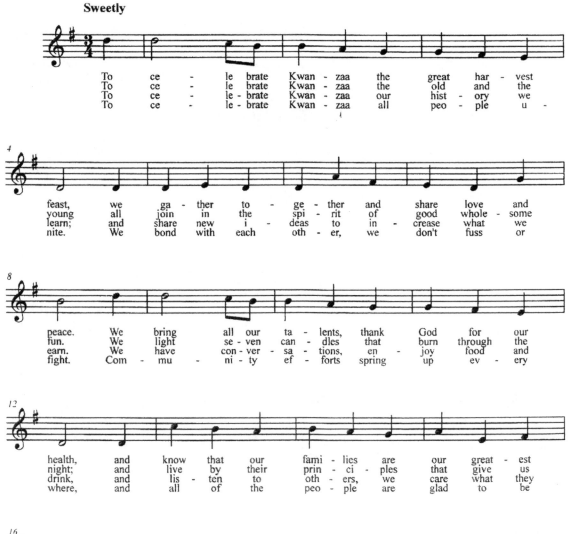

We All Sing of Kwanzaa

Tune: Here We Come A-Wassailing

Lyrics: Karen Griner Smith

Old English

We Are A Race of Honor

Tune: Go Tell It On The Mountain

Lyrics: Karen Griner Smith   Spiritual

We Wish You A Happy Kwanzaa

Tune: We Wish You A Merry Christmas

Lyrics: Karen Griner Smith

Old English

We wish you a Hap-py Kwan-zaa, we wish you a Hap-py Cha U-
Ki - kom - be - Cha U - mo - ja, Ki - kom - be - Cha U -
The straw mat is called M - ke - ka, the straw mat is called M -
Mu - hin - di means ears of dried corn Mu - hin - di means ears of
Ki - na - ra means can - dle hol - der, ki - na - ra means can - dle
Za - wa - di means gifts and pre - sents, Za - wa - di means gifts and
Ka - ra - mu means fun and feast - ing, Ka - ra - mu means fun and

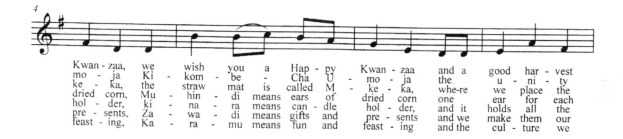

Kwan - zaa, we wish you a Hap - py Kwan - zaa and a good har - vest
mo - ja Ki - kom - be - Cha U - mo - ja the u - ni - ty
ke - ka, the straw mat is called M - ke - ka, whe-re we place the
dried corn, Mu - hin - di means ears of dried corn one ear for each
hol - der, ki - na - ra means can - dle hol - der, and it holds all the
pre - sents, Za - wa - di means gifts and pre - sents and we make them our
feast - ing, Ka - ra - mu means fun and feast - ing and the cul - ture we

feast.   With   heart   felt   Ha - ba - ri   Ga - ni,   with
cup.   Tam - bi - ko   is   the   li - ba - tion,   tam -
things.   Ma - za - o   means fruits of   har - vest   Ma -
child.   We   ce - le - brate past and   pre - sent,   we
lights.   Mishumaa   sa - ba, the   se - ven   can - dles,   Mishumaa
selves.   It   means more than when we buy them,   it
share.   We   dance and   we   sing to   ge - ther   we

We Wish You A Happy Kwanzaa

- Additional Songs with special appeal for young children, set to nursery rhyme tunes with hand clapping, foot stomping, and gestures

- Kwanzaa Raps with special appeal to teens and young adults

- Kwanzaa poems with universal appeal.

Karen Griner Smith

If You Know It's Time for Kwanzaa

Tune: If You're Happy and You Know It

If you know it's time for Kwanzaa clap your hands (clap clap)
If you know it's time for Kwanzaa clap your hands (clap clap)
If your culture you are feeling
Deck your house from floor to ceiling
Kwanzaa time is so appealing clap your hands (clap clap)

If you know it's time for Kwanzaa stomp your feet (stomp stomp)
If you know it's time for Kwanzaa stomp your feet (stomp stomp)
If your culture you are feeling
Deck your house from floor to ceiling
Kwanzaa time is so appealing stomp your feet (stomp stomp)

If you know it's time for Kwanzaa say "Ashe" (a-she)
If you know it's time for Kwanzaa say "Ashe" (a-she)
If your culture you are feeling
Deck your house from floor to ceiling
Kwanzaa time is so appealing say "Ashe" (a-she)

If you know it's time for Kwanzaa laugh out loud (ha-ha)
If you know it's time for Kwanzaa laugh out loud (ha-ha)
If your culture you are feeling
Deck your house from floor to ceiling
Kwanzaa time is so appealing laugh out loud (ha-ha)

If you know it's time for Kwanzaa raise your hands (raise hands, shaking them)
If you know it's time for Kwanzaa raise your hands (raise hands, shaking them)
If your culture you are feeling
Deck your house from floor to ceiling
Kwanzaa time is so appealing raise your hands (raise hands, shaking them)

Why I Love Kwanzaa

Tune: Itsy Bitsy Spider

Why do I love Kwanzaa
Because it's lots of fun.
We all make gifts to
Give to everyone.
We light the candles
And learn our history
And so that's why I love Kwanzaa
Cause it's a time for me.

Why do I love Kwanzaa
Because it gives me pride.
Pride in my people
And proudness deep inside.
Love for myself,
My parents and my friends.
And so that's why I love Kwanzaa
Wish it would never end.

Why do I love Kwanzaa
Because it helps me grow.
Teaching me things
I might not ever know.
Learning from others
In my community
And then seeing all the benefits
Of love and unity.

Karen Griner Smith

Why do I love Kwanzaa
Because for seven days
We light the candles
And eat and talk and play.
African clothes are
What I like to wear
While I celebrate with people
All happy to be there.

Honor to Great People

Tune: The Farmer In the Dell

When Kwanzaa time is here,
When Kwanzaa time is here,
We honor people who are gone
When Kwanzaa time is here.

Shout Martin Luther King.
Shout Martin Luther King.
We honor people who are gone
When Kwanzaa time is here.

Shout out to Malcolm X.
Shout out to Malcolm X.
We honor people who are gone
When Kwanzaa time is here.

For Fredrick Douglas, too.
For Fredrick Douglas, too.
We honor people who are gone
When Kwanzaa time is here.

Shout out to Rosa Parks.
Shout out to Rosa Parks.
We honor people who are gone
When Kwanzaa time is here.

Shout out to Booker T.
Shout out to Booker T.
We honor people who are gone
When Kwanzaa time is here.

For Marcus Garvey, too.
For Marcus Garvey, too.
We honor people who are gone
When Kwanzaa time is here.

Shout out to Willie Mays.
Shout out to Willie Mays.
We honor people who are gone
When Kwanzaa time is here.

Shout out to Emmit Till
Shout out to Emmit Till
We honor people who are gone
When Kwanzaa time is here.

For Coretta Scott King
For Coretta Scott King
We honor people who are gone
When Kwanzaa time is here.

Paul Laurence Dunbar, too.
Paul Laurence Dunbar, too.
We honor people who are gone
When Kwanzaa time is here.

For Adam Clayton Powell
For Adam Clayton Powell
We honor people who are gone
When Kwanzaa time is here.

And Jackie Robinson.
And Jackie Robinson.
We honor people who are gone
When Kwanzaa time is here.

Shout out to Richard Wright
Shout out to Richard Wright
We honor people who are gone
When Kwanzaa time is here.

George Washington Carver
George Washington Carver
We honor people who are gone
When Kwanzaa time is here.

For Ossie Davis, too.
For Ossie Davis, too.
We honor people who are gone
When Kwanzaa time is here.

Shout out to your grandma.
Shout out to your grandma.
We honor people who are gone
When Kwanzaa time is here.

Shout out to your grandpa.
Shout out to your grandpa.
We honor people who are gone
When Kwanzaa time is here.

When Kwanzaa time is here
When Kwanzaa time is here
We honor people who are gone
When Kwanzaa time is here.

Karen Griner Smith

Unity for Kwanzaa

Tune: Row, Row, Row Your Boat

Kwan-zaa time is here
Let's all celebrate!
Unity, unity, unity, unity,
Share, learn and create!

(Sing in round musical style, just like Row, Row, Row Your Boat).

Kwanzaa Rap—Kwanzaa Vibes

Come on in. Take off your coat. Take off your shoes.
We say "Habari Gani" that means, "What's the news?"
To get down with this good time home grown Kwanzaa thing
You got to open your heart and let your spirit sing.
All day and night, yeah Kwanzaa's tight!

Kwanzaa is mad nice. The vibe is fresh and snappy.
It's when you feeling cool because your hair is nappy.
The time's about us raisin' up our faith and our hope
And putting down the guns and saying nope to dope.
Like having seven whole days of heaven.

At Kwanzaa time the vibe is cool. The vibe is sharing.
The Kwanzaa jam is fun. The juice is love and caring.
The Kwanzaa energy is on a positive tip
'Cause doing stuff for your peeps is doing stuff that's hip
We dig each other, sisters and brothers.

It's all about creating stuff and us having faith
To use our minds and skills to do whatever it takes.
The Kwanzaa vibe is us believing unity
Will make a better life in our community.
All peeps respected; no one neglected.

For seven days and seven nights this time each year
Your family and friends come 'round from far and near
To eat up Mama's chicken and potato salad
And listen to your cousin Mookie sing a ballad.
Laughing and joking, Kwanzaa is smoking.

At Kwanzaa time the vibe is very hip and clean.
It's all about us boosting up our self-esteem.
It's not about the bling but about self-affirmation.
And there is just no time for beefing and aggravation.
Kwanzaa has flavor that you can savor.

Kwanzaa Rap—Black Man's Burden

Hey now don't forget, yes everyone remember
Beginning on the 26th day of December
It's time to get the Kwanzaa candles burning bright
To kick it with our peeps for seven days and nights.
And every single night we pour out the libation
In memory of those who led to our creation
We got to give a shout out and send love and praise
To all the ones who are gone in these good Kwanzaa days.
Never neglect to show respect.

The middle passage was the black man's holocaust.
Some made it to the shores but thousands more were lost.
The ones who made it here, they got the whip and chains
They lost all that they had; they even lost their names
But both their spirits and their backs were strong
And they learned to survive by singing Godly songs.
We need to give respect for their great sacrifice,
For giving all of us a legacy for life.
A legacy for you and me.

We need to thank the ones who helped to build this land,
Who slaved all day and night and made stuff with their hands.
The ones who worked the fields and those that worked in the house.
The ones who ran away and those who stayed in the south.
The ones that went to school and got an education
And kicked the knowledge to us for a firm foundation,
Like Frederick Douglas, Malcolm, Martin Luther King
And all the peeps that taught us how to do our thing.
Praise to the ones who got things done

Remembering the grandmas cooking our favorite dish;
Remembering the grandpas teaching us how to fish.
The way they made a little bit seem like it's a lot.
The way they made plain stuff seem like it was something hot.
The way they sat the shorties down upon their lap
And gave us lots of love while giving serious rap;
For all the stuff our ancestors had to go through,
To give up much respect is what we aught to do.
It was rough, but they did their stuff.

Kwanzaa Rap—Bop

You hear the drumming (clap, clap) cause Kwanzaa's coming (clap, clap).

Now can you handle (clap, clap) the seven candles? (clap, clap).

We all be learning (clap, clap) to increase earning (clap, clap)

Go pass the surface (clap, clap) to learn our purpose (clap, clap).

We don't talk trash (clap, clap) We earn some cash! (clap, clap)

No time to waste (clap, clap) we seek our faith (clap, clap)

We get with neighbors (clap, clap) to help with labors (clap, clap)

We don't be hating (clap, clap) We be creating. (clap, clap).

It ain't the blinging (clap, clap) It's 'bout the singing (clap, clap).

Back in the kitchen (clap, clap) they frying chicken (clap, clap).

Just to be pleasant (clap, clap) we make some presents. (clap, clap).

Nobody's illing. (clap, clap) We all be chilling. (clap, clap).

Peeps all be viben. (clap, clap) And we high fiven (clap, clap).

All day and night, (clap, clap). Yeah Kwanzaa's tight! (clap, clap).

Practice Kwanzaa Everyday

Don't forget, always remember
January to December
See if you can find a way to
Practice Kwanzaa everyday.

Kwanzaa principles help us
Not to fear or fight or fuss.
They help us to work together
Making life for all much better.

Every day of every week
Of every month we all should seek
To become better people and
To try to help our fellowman.

Practice Kwanzaa all year long.
It will make our people strong.
Through our self-determination
We will make a better nation.

Practicing this love and peace
Negativity will cease.
Everyone will show they care.
Principles will lead us there.

Karen Griner Smith

Kwanzaa Poem

It's time for Kwanzaa
For seven whole days
We celebrate us
In our own special way.

The first fruits of harvest
Do greatly abound
There's joy in the air-
Friends and family come around.

Place down the straw mat
And then ears of corn
Each one represents that
A child has been born.

Then place the vegetables
Spread fruits and nuts
To show the abundance
That's given to us.

There's a unity cup.
Come pour the libation,
And then take a sip
For the strength of our nation.

We place the kinara
It has seven spaces
To put all the candles
In just the right places.

One candle is black.
Three red and three green.
One is lit every night;
And here is what they mean:

The black's for our people
The red is for our blood
The green's for the land
From which we all come.

We place simple gifts
On the straw mat as well.
Then share with each other
We have stories to tell.

We sing and we dance
We come out to praise
Our present, our future
And rich heritage.

We all celebrate
Black community
And speak principles
That promote unity.

We have pot luck meals
We all share the food
That everyone brings
And it always is good.

9 781468 541403